930

D0727497

Titles in this series
Big J
Clever Cleo
Don't Say No To Flo
Gunpowder Guy
Hal the Hero
The Little Queen
Will's Dream
William's Words

Text copyright © Stewart Ross 2001
Illustrations copyright © Sue Shields 2001

Series concept: Stewart Ross
Series editor: Alex Woolf
Editor: Liz Gogerly
Book Design: Design Systems

The Publisher would like to thank AKG, London for kind permission to use the picture on page 30. This Egyptian limestone relief shows Cleopatra as Isis.

Published in Great Britain by Hodder Wayland, an imprint of Hodder Children's Books

A catalogue record for this book is available from the British Library.

ISBN 0 7502 2853 9

Printed in Hong Kong

Hodder Children's Books
A division of Hodder Headline Limited
338 Euston Road, London NW1 3BH

Clever Cleo

Stewart Ross
Illustrated by Sue Shields

HODDER
Wayland
an imprint of Hodder Children's Books

Old King Pot ...

... had two children.

Tiny Tolly had beefy friends.

Cleo was clever and beautiful.

Old King Pot talked to Tolly and Cleo.

He wanted them to be king and queen.

Soon the old king died.

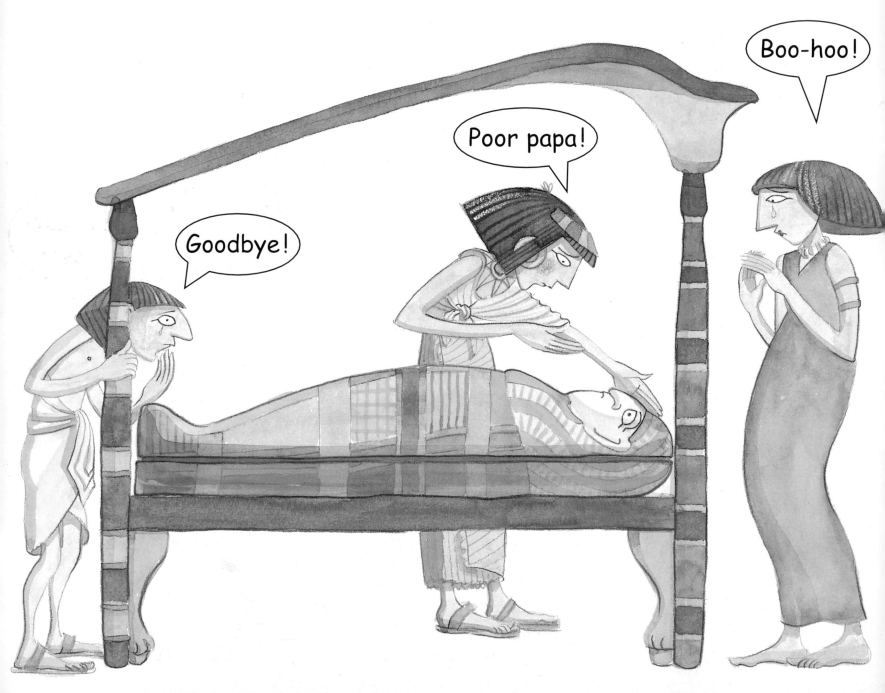

Tolly and Cleo were king and queen.

They did not get on.

Tolly's beefy friends did not like Cleo.

Just then ...

... Jules the super soldier arrived.

Cleo wanted to meet Jules.

Go to Jules. Say I want to meet him.

Yes, Cleo.

But Jules did not want to meet Cleo.

Cleo had a clever idea.

The men carried Cleo to Jules' palace.

Jules and Cleo met.

Soon they were very good friends.

Jules said he would help his new friend.

Jules' soldiers had a fight ...

... with Tolly's beefy friends.

Tolly's beefy friends ran away.

Jules came back to the palace.

So Tolly and Cleo ...

... were king and queen again.

Do you know?

This story is TRUE!

Cleo was CLEOPATRA. Jules was JULIUS CAESAR. Tolly was PTOLEMY.

CLEOPATRA lived more than 2,000 years ago.

She died in 30 BC.

This is what she looked like:

Notes for adults

Clever Cleo and the National Curriculum

Clever Cleo may be enjoyed in its own right or, in school, as part of a programme of reading and study linked to the National Curriculum. To this end, the language, content and presentation have been devised to meet the requirements of the National Literacy Strategy and Key Stage 1 English and History. Whether read by an individual pupil or by the teacher out loud, *Clever Cleo* makes a stimulating addition to material available for the Literacy Hour. It combines development of the 'knowledge, skills and understanding' and 'breadth of study' required by the English National Curriculum (pp. 18-19) with 'chronological understanding', 'knowledge and understanding of events, people and changes in the past' and learning about 'the lives of significant men, women and children drawn from the history of Britain and the wider world' and 'past events from the history of Britain and the wider world' suggested in the History National Curriculum (p.16).

Suggested follow-up activities

1. Checking the child knows and can use words they might not have come across before. In particular:

Tolly	goodbye	soldiers	minute
Cleo	thanks	palace	ouch
clever	anything	idea	dear
Jules	carried	wait	easy
beautiful	super	meow	fight
wanted	dead	beefy	

2. Talking about pictures of tangible objects that survive from ancient Egyptian civilization, e.g. buildings (Sphinx, Pyramids etc.), mummies and everyday objects such as jewellery.

3. Discussing how we know about Egyptian civilization, i.e. sources (perhaps looking at hieroglyphs).

4. Explaining the exact dates of Cleopatra's reign, and the meaning of BC and AD dates.

5. Going further into aspects of Egyptian civilization, e.g. religion, gods and goddesses, the importance of the Nile, pharaohs, architecture, links with other ancient civilizations, e.g. Exodus, the full story of Cleopatra, etc.

6. Comparing life in Egyptian times with our own, e.g. clothing, health and disease, travel, housing, warfare, religion, etc.